CW00585043

Light from the Upper Left

Bob Cooper
Jo Haslam

Smith/Doorstop Books

Published 1994 by
Smith/Doorstop Books
The Poetry Business
The Studio
Byram Arcade
Westgate
Huddersfield HD1 1ND

ISBN 1 869961 45 5

Typeset at The Poetry Business
Printed by Swiftprint, Huddersfield

Cover by the blue door design company, Heckmondwike

Distributed by Password (Books) Ltd.,
23 New Mount Street, Manchester M4 4DE

The Poetry Business gratefully acknowledges
the help of Kirklees Metropolitan Council and
Yorkshire & Humberside Arts.

Thanks are due to the editors of the following publications in
which some of these poems have been previously published:
Staple; *Smoke*; *Smiths Knoll*; *A Different Can of Words*; *Fat
Chance*; *Poems 93* (Lancaster Lit. Fest. Comp.)

Bob Cooper's first pamphlet, *Bruised Echoes*, was published
by Stride in 1977.

CONTENTS

Bob Cooper

Jo Haslam

Clean Hands

Bob Cooper

MAN AND BOY

Squeezed bales hiss down the chute,
creaking piles lugged from the sled.
They stop to drink, check the twine;
petrol, sweat, dust, sweeten the air.

'We'll finish this field tonight, start
the next tomorrow.'   The farmer grins,
'How's married life?'   Youth spits,
stares at his shadow's length, 'Alright.'

Bootless feet in the scullery
while his wife pours tea,
'I thought it kicked this afternoon;'
water burns his neck and arms.

CALVING AND THE OU

He's been out twice.
This time he stays until
gradually it appears,
its dark weight easing out.
Then the final thrust
slithering onto straw.
Labia close like covers
on a well-read book.

He's seen this so often.
Knelt in this silence,
encouraging; his wonder
spoken in soothing words.
Then the huge head sways in,
laps the placenta.
He pulls on his coat,
crosses the yard. It's done.

In front of the fire
his wife sleeps,
text-book on her lap:
Socrates' maeutic method ...
Gently he tugs it,
closes it. She wakes;
laughing they yawn,
talk of births.

THE WOODMAN'S DAUGHTER

The earth is pale, dry;
frost glistens on leaves, stone.
As the coffin is lowered
she gazes at trees.

*

He'd been planting ash,
found her mum in the bedroom;
ran down the lane,
knocked on their neighbour's door,
'Baby's on its way,
will you feed the hens?'

He finished the story,
put her down,
looked at the saplings
and smiled.

*

Wood was soothing;
the click of cupboards,
creak of stairs.
Calm as chairs and table,
it shone.

Seeing a tree being butchered;
stretched like a pig,
roots like entrails
hung in the air.
Her father smiled,

tugged down his cap
as the chain-saw roared.

She ran home howling,
stumbled upstairs.
Looked at the wardrobe,
at the knots and whorls
on the tongue of dead wood.

*

She'd heard the pleading,
the door's slam;
'Down to the river, to drown.'
He put logs on the fire,
pulled on his coat,
'Don't cry, keep warm.'

The room was cold.
'No more custard or scones
without Mum.'
She stared at the grate,
the spurting flame gnawing,
catching hold.

When the door opened
they both came inside,
flakes melting in their hair.
They took her to bed.
Snow sloughed off the branches,
twigs slender again.

*

She remembers him splitting logs;
right arm raised,
crooked, then sliding
a long silent curve
that ended in applause.

Calloused fingers around the lamp;
trimming the wick,
striking the match,
replacing the glass.
Satisfied in the glow.

Him pointing,
'Look, there,
a shooting star.'
Hens shuffled on their perch
as he closed the door.

*

As the coffin is lowered
she gazes at trees;
the age he was at her birth
planting ash,
planting oak.

ON THE ALLOTMENT

The door, fringed with peeling paint,
judders, springs open,
releasing tomatoes' pungence
thickened green by night.
His jacket, hung like onions,
weights the nail. Pockets bulge
with secateurs, biscuits, twine.
He tips the watering can, fingers marrows,
hums what his daughter is learning at school.

BACK LANE, ALTOFTS

Watching the moon,
huge as an elm,
while the canal rubs its edge
against narrow gardens,
the scent of stocks drifts down.

Pigeons murmur in allotment sheds,
a motorcycle barks;
he strikes a match,
the sweet smoke blown
from his mouth to the moon.

Fingers burrow
deep in his hand
and his chuckle,
dark, slow as water,
'Aye lass, time for thi' bed.'

LIGHT PROGRAMME

Click. A hum
and from its depths a glow.
The gabbled swirls – up, down –
as the needle crossed STUTTGART, BREMEN,
strange voices, HILVERSUM.
Brian Johnston in Sydney, static, applause,
Wilfred Pickles in Hunslet, HAVE A GO.
After JOURNEY INTO SPACE a blood moon rose.
Later the air was dark with voices – rising, falling.
I crept back down, paused,
opened the door. In strident light
they stood in mid-word. 'I was worried
about the Spacemen captured on Mars.'
From down-under I heard the score.

Bob Cooper

THE APPLE TREE

At each swing slivers flew,
niches deepened, until we pushed
and it swayed, tore itself, fell.
But there was no rejoicing.

Each year blossom darkened the room;
fruit hung on brittle twigs
screeching across glass.
Now we drank tea, again sweated hard,

sawed logs, split their crispness,
stacked them. They gleamed,
burned fiercely, exploding sparks.
We watched the rug, anxious.

Later, when the stump was fired,
consuming the heart,
we knew roots remained, nudging brick.
We would still have to dig.

Bob Cooper

AFTER THE SHOOT

The Keeper counts, 'Thirtyfour brace';
partridge, pheasant, laid in lines.
Dogs nuzzle or lope at ease.
Beaters hand out cans of beer.
Laughter rises as ring-pulls crack,
best wishes for the New Year.

Game's smell is wiped from hands,
guns, birds, slung in car boots
while an owl ghosts between trees,
the sky huge with Orion.

CHARON

You get used to this job; the warmth,
dry smell; it's mainly routine.
Each morning, mop floors, shake mats;
unlock glass, turn a page in the book;
select tapes – Bach's Jesu Joy, Crimond,
Handel's Largo, though some bring their own.
Then listen for the cue as you glance
over form at Lingfield until curtains, music,
lean over the trolley, open the hatch.

But today the cassette played through
and they were still filing in.
The drivers, out back for a smoke,
tight-lipped. And as they all left,
when I pulled it through
I could have lifted it, carried it
like a fragile present. But
I still did as I usually do.

Bob Cooper

WALKING PAST THE LOCK

Sluice gates open,
the cut fills with sound;
water plunges, rises like loss
finding its level.

Reflections settle
and you move on;
hear meadow-larks,
stare up at what you can't see.

SUNDAY MORNING

As if children lived at home
he pads upstairs with tea;
curtains unopened, sheets lifted,
musk, a stain, nightdress still raised,
warmth. They sip. 'H'm', is all
that's said, is all that need be said
as a clock chimes, slow as hearts,
sun dapples the wall; a sense
that such as this is wasted on the young.

Bob Cooper

SEEING THE WOOD

Yesterday, after frost,
as sunlight soaked the lawn,
drenched colour onto brick,
the ash tree emptied itself.
Neighbours' maple, cherry, beech,
linger, kaleidoscope for weeks,
but ash just shrugs off leaves,
discards them to grass.

This morning, branches bare,
I see bedroom windows, pale slates,
contrails dabbed across a wash of sky
and can't forget last night; an owl's call
as I lay, aware of nothing else
but the cold. That's how it is
in October: raw sounds, staring at things
like grey twigs unaccustomed to light.

THE STOCKMAN

The hosepipe jerked, stiffened;
piss and disinfectant frothed,
whitened where the yardbrush scraped.
Cows watched, clattered metal bars.

'Gerron, yer bastards. Gerron.'
Slow-necked they swayed, slavering,
shit-thighed. He lifted the sneck;
cows lumbered, calves scattered through.

Children, wife, upped and gone;
behind bottles, plates stared from the mat;
around the fire damp shirts hung.
He gripped the mirror's edge, heard lino lift.

He was found by the Stock Feed Salesman,
stained pyjamas crumpled in the byre.
Cows trampled, bellowed in the slurry.
The Coroner's Open Verdict: 'Three days.'

Bob Cooper

TWO-TONE SHOES

Today, she's told, someone called
Julie will wash her hair.
Beyond screens, tall windows,
the wind tugs, undresses trees.
It was windy the day she slipped.
She wonders who found her,
phoned later, left flowers,

then hears Val with the tea-trolley,
the tune from the television news.
Albert will visit this afternoon;
four hours travelling, two by the bed,
with more wool, complaints, glances
at each bruise, while she'll stare
at the bouquet he hasn't yet noticed

and recall the man who said much
in few words, dried her face,
gathered her jars, packets of tea,
took off his coat in the rain.
But his name … his name?
He wore socks with a rose on the side,
two-tone shoes.

REMINISCENCE GROUP

She no longer fidgets but talks
of wartime when she'd built stone walls:

'Working, daybreak till your back breaks,'
she laughs, 'How we ached;

bending, selecting, chipping, laying;
sat out of the wind eating damsons, bacon.

Home for the weekend, a bath;
at the Pictures: Tyrone Power, George Raft.

The best time?   Early April
when you'd hear a curlew's call:

'I've returned', it sang, 'I've returned.'
She rubs lichen off clean hands.

Proofs

Jo Haslam

SNOW

It was the slightest touch against his shoulder
that made him turn. Snow, coming from behind,
cold January, a heavy sky.
She saw the shoulders of his tweed
sports jacket, powdered white.
A crystal blurring on his lashes
as he looked up and said
'More to come tonight.'

Already it was thickening
blowing round their heads and deadening all noise,
except for their voices calling through the drifting flakes.
If she had known then, the cold that would reach out to him
she would have shouted till her heart had burst,
unfrozen him with quick warm breath
as she had blown away so easily the snow
that settled on his mouth and eyelids.

But they have irreversibly altered
the shape of his mouth, packed his flesh
hard white. She cannot make a sound.
Cold has set within her
a stone of ice nothing can melt.

BIRDS FLY SOUTH.

Birds fly south, on lines of barometric pressure.
They travel flyways, Atlantic and Pacific, enormous distances
across oceans, mountain ranges, to Africa, to South
America. In some mythologies
they sleep on the wing
not stopping for food or water.

From great altitudes they scan landscape,
features, hills and rivers; take bearings from
the stars and sun, or are pulled
by the earth's magnetic field.
They travel day and night,
the Arctic Tern performing yearly a round trip
of twenty-three thousand miles.

It's said that they are prompted by a shortening
of daylight, drops in temperature and food supplies
diminishing. But what impels their urgent
flight can only be guessed at.

Likewise other phenomena that baffle understanding:
fish in shoals that shift as one,
plankton rising from great depths
to the surface, salmon coursing from freshwater
to open seas, or reindeer crossing snowy wastes
summoned by something
they had heard that we had not.

The Aborigines who in the Dreamtime sang
their stones into existence have an explanation
as good as any other. They say they walked
and sang to make their landscape visible

and must trace their Dreamlines still, not erase
the created world of God.

So let us sleep and cross our night latitudes.
Let us dream the birds, sleeping as they navigate.
(It does not matter if they dream us or not.)
With one mind they'll up, tremendous flocks,
and fly without diverting

straight to where they divine warmth,
shade where it is needed, water and food in plenty;
calm breeding grounds, some paradise.
Let us dream the birds flying above us
sleeping on the wing,
not stopping for food or water.
Let us dream the birds flying along lines of barometric pressure
who, when they reach their resting place, sing.

Jo Haslam

THE SIGN FOR WATER

He makes the sign for water.
She makes the sign for fish.
His movement fluid from the shoulder.
Hers swifter, starting from the wrist,

thumb uppermost, cutting the air
like the quick flick tailing fish
through water. They meet,
his hands slide over hers

and it is there almost as if he' d drawn
the three lines of the hieroglyph
that we know for certain denote liquid,
ocean, waves. And as she draws

the letters on his palm, and he
makes out the word-shape with his lips,
the whole hydraulic motion of the earth
rolls under them.

So my deaf child to his lover
speaking without sound,
hands closing the air between her meaning
and his profound lack of hearing.

He crosses his two hands
over the place he knows
his heart to be, and when he holds
the cupped palms out then we

expect to see it pulse
between them. So will they touch and speak
all their life over and over,
his lover, my deaf child,

their mutual dialogue
silent and complete. Their love's
language has no rules.
They leap it as the silver

leaping fish. What are they talking of
now? Miracles or loaves,
it does not matter as he makes the sign for fish
and she makes the sign for water.

Jo Haslam

JOURNEY

Going there you fell asleep, head to one side.
Your face had that bleached look
of one who was very tired, or ill.
But you slept, almost as if
you were entering a period of recovery.

We in the front seats could not think ahead
only of what was immediate –
how many miles to go before our destination
newspapers we had left behind and other things
that we might need – small change for parking …

I watched you in the mirror.
You'd slept like this before, rocked
by the motion of a train or car.
At those journeys' ends I'd lift you on my shoulder,
your body solid and hot, skin like a crumpled petal.

Now you unfold long limbs, ease your legs
from the back seat, shake your trouser crease,
look up. It is raining, cold drops
out of the morning sky, blotching the street.
At the door, going in, no time for goodbye,
you stopped, just once, suddenly to kiss me and I
began to cry.

RIDDLE

What was it that you were?
You were all of these things:
You were a fragile face I had
to hold between my hands
to stop it from disintegrating.
You were a boy with sunlight
on his flaky skin.
You were a terrible deep wound.
You were someone I could confuse
with someone else,
a man whose stomach troubled him.
You were a baby who would not stop crying.

You were very small, hard as a pebble.
You were larva soft, you were tall
then small again, tall with a flapping coat
dark with a white skin, your hands were cold.
You were someone like my brother
or my child. You were the one
I could never write about.

Now, I cloak you in words.
They print your skin like kisses,
crosses, thin as tissue, as my pen,
they fold, stroke, the bruised
dark patch below your eyes,
they link your dry cold hands with mine.

You are that one, the heavy weight inside,
the leaf-like nervous flutter

where my stomach hollowed.
And in each case you are an ache,
a fragile face, a boy
with flaky skin, short sighted,
someone, like my brother,
or my son, a child who in the night
I am still listening for,
a baby who will not stop crying.

SNOW SPACES

They seem enormous these snow spaces
but they are measurable by footsteps between them,
man, woman, child.
She is in midstep and counting.
The picture freezes.

I searched for a snow picture I had lost,
at first couldn't see one.
Distance then was judged by how far away she was.
A street's length between us was much greater than the distance
between star, sand and snowflake.
The fear that she would disappear if I looked away.

But it comes back suddenly – a huge midnight sky,
ground sparking hard with frost and a million sparking echoes
in the sky as we looked up. And what dizzied us was not
their vibrant pulsing, or unimaginable distances –
they seemed no distance from us –
but that there seemed to be no difference
between them and us and the terrestrial frost we stood on.
How could they be suns, those icy splinters?
We'd felt their freezing touch on our upturned faces.

The last one – snow falls and stills to dazzling white
I want to show you each unique revolving world,
the enormous spaces in between and how they cross.
You draw a breath and wail into the freezing air.
I lift you up and touch your burning cheeks
and holding you we break across
and with our footprints mark the snow's dazzling white gulf.

Jo Haslam

SWIFTS

Swifts in the air sleep
while their wings are still at work.
Dropping in and out of catnaps
they copulate, cavort
and still in flight zoom in
on aerial plankton, flying insects,
spiders that spin past
in the razor blue.

Undeterred by thinning air, they swoop
and climb, as if just launched
from a trapeze, lifting on an impossible vertical –
move in a dimension of their own,
through clouds, wind currents, past
invisible tectonic plates
of close and spinning life:
dart and hover, improvise
tumble and drop almost to the ground, then shoot up
as if they could not bear the loss of altitude,

inhabiting the upper air for years
until the urge to nest and reproduce
draws them to the earth,
which they come at from the side
as if the buildings trees and mountains
had all moved and laid themselves out flat
beneath their feet
and rivers had swung out to meet them
gleaming and upright like wardrobe mirrors.
They swerve into them and emerge in sunlight
dripping but still flapping.

LIGHTHOUSE

After they have set his teeth on edge
one with his constant shuffling of cards
the other with whistling, just under his breath,
he takes a turn about the lighthouse rock.

He has occupied himself till now
perfecting practical things,
learning the rules of Mah Jong
and how to cook crème brulée

sauté potatoes, crèpes frosted with sugar,
and they have to admit he's good
even when it's difficult to get the right
ingredients – he'll improvise,

it shakes the boredom off and the moods
that settle on him when he looks across
the miles between the lighthouse
and dry land. Waves lift here sometimes

thirty feet high, and the smur comes in,
the sea wave's breath invades the rock
and they come back, stories he has read
of lost, wrecked ships, cries

of the dead, that sound under water
hollows where the seaweed moves
coral crusted eye-sockets
and the man with his two legged bride

Jo Haslam

who walks with her upright
but wakes at night to find the cold smell
of the sea inside their room
walls washed by a green light

scales of silver on his hands.
And though he knows that there are seven
seas that cover seven tenths
of the earth's surface, that they were once

the place we dreamed and dwelt in
and that they have the strength still
to devour and cleanse, he is
a man who cannot swim and it would

seem sensible of him to fear drowning
the white honing on the ocean floor
never to float up or be discovered.
And other stories he has heard

each one fabulous and strange, dolphins
bearing exhausted travellers
to the shore, seals who shed their skins
assume human shape and dance. Jonah

swallowed and spewed up from the maw
of the leviathan. But he still prays
the lord deliver him, this time, always
from these, and similar encounters.

Jo Haslam

PROOF

The smell of you is on your clothes
even though they have been washed
and folded in the drawer
since you have been away.

Your brother took a shirt out the other day
and wears it now continually.
The cuffs hang down below his wrists
the hemline to his knees. He says
that you gave him permission. Your jacket,
shirts, sweaters that are probably
too small. When he is at school
I wash them. Arms and chest billow
on the line and still the smell of you clings,
much more strongly to the wool
than to your other clothes.

De-pilling them,
I gathered up the little matted tufts
and rolled them in a ball, forgot them
till the cat discovered one and chased it
without warning, pounced, and we
all jumped, thinking it was something else
just like the time when someone knocked:
the door flew open suddenly,
my head jerked up,
my heart almost stopped.

Jo Haslam

DIVING BELL

I thought of them, the four little ones
who died while sailing out to India
that year, what was it?
Well before the war anyway,
the small packages swaddled, sealed
and slipped overboard. That one
your mother's story.

Another one: your father bringing
his brother out of the water, not dead quite
but changed. He told us how he never
could get over that white face, the closed
pebble veined eyes; and always
when looked at from the side
that queer iridescence.

And in Ireland one holiday
a whole boatload gone down
and on the harbour an absolute quiet
as they waited for the news.
Your aunt in the kitchen just before,
the slap of dough on the board,
a film of flour dusting her hands.

And it came back, St Martin's Eve
when eighty men went down,
whole families and friends – all these
when hearing of the ship
that foundered in the dark, and the men
inside the diving bell that came to rest
on the ocean floor. For days

40

it was repeated in the newspapers
until they said there was
no hope of finding anyone alive.
And I thought of all that weight of ocean,
strange plant life, unknown pollution, the cold
indifferent salt water; and none of it
we knew for certain could corrode

the sealed chamber that held them,
seven men, dead drowned divers,
underneath the dark sea
closed above the diving bell.
Was it just the claustrophobic's dread
that made me wish for their release
into the water's interminable scouring?

No strangers there, they'd known
the different movement, weight,
how to compute
the pressure on each square inch
that gave them tenure; how deep
the water and how far and strange
as any cold dead star. This too:

just like the first breath-holding divers
who risked deafness, sometimes their lives
plunging for pearl or sponge.
And we as much as they,
all divers still,
resume what was our element
as aliens, observers, predators

and lovers too. We trawl and reach
sea depths where sunlight never penetrates
reefs of coral, fish that lose colour
as they swim deeper, to close at last
on treasures, miracles of pearl
and surface or fall
and fall into the ocean.

VISITOR

Already your ghost has come
and greets me from your chair –
this one smooth-skinned and clear-eyed.
But others follow him
crowd into the room, polymorphous,
confident or diffident but none
of them respecters of time
place or occasion.

Sometimes just the one, like this
my late night visitor
with his confident grin,
ghost of my imagining. He has chosen
a good day.
Another time he could be beaten,
changed, beyond anything
that I could alter.

And this is just a beginning.
I must contend with all his
former ghosts and those who wait
for him to catch up with them.
He does not know yet which one
he will choose.

But for me now no
ghost further than this one
goes into the future.

Jo Haslam

PROOFS

The plate's been burred, the whole of it
minutely pitted so the ink will hold,
and it would print now deepest black.
But with the same intent as that
which has brought the technique
from the eighteenth century to now
I'll smooth the image back.
Mezzotint, coming slowly into the light.

Out of the tones, the half tones and the dark,
'nature mort', still life, flowers, chair
a bowl of fruit, a square table top.
And I think of how it is like daybreak,
this return from blackness that revoked terra firma.
And how I'll reach for all that has been left the night before
to feel that they are solid there, my proofs
as they take shape out of the first paling grey.
And it begins, the intimate decoding of the universe:
a plate, a chair, flowers where they were
turning from violet to crimson.

WATCHING THE BIRDS

You told me how you watched the flight of birds
from your window. You whose every movement
is confined. Although you did not say
from which direction they had come, or
in what weather, sky or time of day, or even
what kind of bird; gulls coming inland
or smaller birds swooping over fields to pick
between the stubble. Only that their flight,
their movement seemed to you an image
of infinite freedom. And it's true – we have always
taken them – phoenix, dove , swan –
as symbols of regeneration, peace and fidelity, fidelis.
But you know of course that they come down to scavenge
feed, rest, rear their young. And that their life is short.

Once, I caught an injured bird, felt its pulse
against my chest. Felt the strangeness of its soft
under-feathers, its alive warmth, all its muscle
sinewy, bony, webbed and feathery wings, quivering, pulsing
darting, eyes and beak, all at once and all in one,
cupped in my hand. And though we have not talked yet
of caged birds, you know that you have reared one
who beats against my ribs, furiously and painfully.

DREAMTIME

In someone else's Dreamtime, this had already happened.
In someone else's Dreamtime this was already waiting
complete and finished
for you to stumble on it.
In someone else's Dreamtime, this had already happened.
But not in ours.

Still, once brought from under the earth's crust
it cannot be undreamed.
It must stand with all the other things that have been dreamed
into existence; guns and instruments of torture,
famine, war, our world-destroying bombs
and individual miseries.

We can only challenge them with our own Dreamtimes.
This is mine –
a small town we pass fortnightly.
A river with green banking on one side.
On the other a pale wall of stone.
Boats knock against this wall

all summer and the water flashes, blue-silver
in the sun. It does not rain here in our Dreamtime.
This is where we will go one day.
You will teach your brother to row.
Already I can see your laughing face.
Your father has dreamt it also. It will happen.

Jo Haslam

MOUTH OF FRUIT

Your mouth has the chill of the smooth inside of fruit
we leave all night on the window sill.
Fruit in a blue bowl
melon, pear and green and yellow apples.
In the morning, cold has left a dull film
a white breath on it.
Selecting one piece, you rub it on your sleeve
and warm it at the fire,
rolling it from hand to hand.
Your fingers glow, transparent, pink.
You roll the apple down your palms
finger tip to finger tip.
The apple skin becomes satiny.
At last you bite and leave four white grooves against the green.
You say inside it's very cold.
It sets your teeth on edge. Only the skin
is warm. The heat of the fire has not
penetrated. You eat it though,
the whole of it, apple skin, flesh and pip.
At night it lingers on your kiss, the smell
of apple, and on your mouth the chill
of the smooth inside of fruit.

Bob Cooper and **Jo Haslam** are joint winners of The Poetry Business Competition 1993.

Bob Cooper was born on Teesside in 1950. He is a Methodist Minister formerly in Warrington and now on Tyneside. He also climbs rocks.

Jo Haslam was born in 1947. She studied painting, and now works as a freelance illustrator and designer. She has been writing for seven years. She lives in Marsden with one husband, five cats, one dog and varying numbers of children.

For full details of the current Competition, our books and cassettes, and *The North* magazine, send a stamped addressed envelope to **The Poetry Business, The Studio, Byram Arcade, Westgate, Huddersfield HD1 1ND**

Smith/Doorstop Books

publish books, cassettes
and pamphlets by

Moniza Alvi	Jo Haslam
Simon Armitage	Geoff Hattersley
Sujata Bhatt	Jeanette Hattersley
Liz Cashdan	Keith Jafrate
Julia Casterton	Mimi Khalvati
Debjani Chatterjee	John Lancaster
Bob Cooper	Peter Lane
Tim Cumming	John Lyons
Duncan Curry	Ian McMillan
Peter Daniels	Cheryl Martin
Joyce Darke	Paul Matthews
Owen Davis	Eleanor Maxted
Carol Ann Duffy	David Morley
Anna Fissler	Les Murray
Sophie Hannah	Lemn Sissay
John Harvey	Mary Woodward